Bread and Fish

Based on Mark 6:30–46 and John 6:5–14

By Mrs. Marvin Good

Illustrated by Lester M. Miller

Rod and Staff Publishers, Inc.
P.O. Box 3, Hwy. 172
Crockett, Kentucky 41413
Telephone: (606) 522-4348

SAY-IT-AGAIN SERIES

Bread and Fish
Daniel in the Lions' Den
David and Goliath
The Good Samaritan
How God Made the World
My Book About Bartimaeus
A Shepherd Boy

These books were written to provide simple, repetitious stories to be read by beginning readers who can profit by the extra repetition, or to be read to younger children whose minds can more readily grasp the content of oft-repeated material.

Copyright, 1993
By
Rod and Staff Publishers, Inc.
Crockett, Kentucky 41413

Printed in U.S.A.
ISBN 978-07399-0007-9
Catalog no. 2397

The disciples came to Jesus.
They came to talk to Jesus.
They came to tell Jesus what they did.

Jesus said, "Come. Come to the desert. Come to the desert and rest."

A ship.

Jesus and the disciples got on a ship.

They got on a ship to go to the desert.

The people saw the ship.
They saw the ship leave.
The people wanted Jesus.
They wanted to be with Jesus.

The people ran.
They ran fast.
They got to the landing before Jesus did.

Jesus saw all the people.
He saw many people.
The people looked sad.
Jesus felt sorry for the people.

Jesus spoke.

He spoke to the people.

He spoke about God.

He spoke many things about God.

The disciples came to Jesus.
They came to Jesus and said,
"This is a desert.
It is evening.
The people need bread."

The disciples said, "Send the people away.
Send them to the country.
Send them to the village.
Send them so that they can buy bread."

Jesus said to the disciples,
"Give them bread.
Give them bread to eat."

The disciples asked,
"Should we go buy bread?
Should we go buy much bread?
We need much bread for so many people."

Andrew said, "A lad is here.

The lad has loaves.
The lad has fishes.

"The lad has 5 loaves. He has 5 barley loaves. The lad has 2 fishes. He has 5 loaves and 2 fishes.

"That is not enough.

That is not enough for so many people.

What shall we do?"

Jesus said, "Tell the people to sit.

Tell them to sit down."

The people sat down.

They sat on the grass.

There were many people.

There were many, many people.

Many people sat on the grass.

Five thousand people sat on the grass.

Jesus took the loaves.
He took the barley loaves.
Jesus thanked God.
He thanked God for the bread.

Jesus gave bread.

He gave bread to the disciples.

He gave lots of bread to the disciples.

The disciples gave bread.

The disciples gave bread to the people.

The people ate.

They ate lots of bread.

Jesus took the fish.
He took the 2 fish.
Jesus thanked God.
He thanked God for the fish.

Jesus gave fish.

He gave fish to the disciples.

He gave lots of fish to the disciples.

The disciples gave fish.

The disciples gave fish to the people.

The people ate.

They ate until they had enough.

Jesus said, "Gather what is left.

Gather the bread and the fishes.

Do not waste any of it."

The disciples gathered the bread.

They gathered the fish.

Nothing was left.

Nothing was left on the ground.

The disciples filled 1 basket.

The disciples filled 2 baskets.

They filled 3 baskets.

They filled more baskets and more baskets.

The disciples filled 12 baskets.

The people saw the miracle.
They saw the miracle Jesus did.
The people said, "Jesus is a prophet."

"Many . . . are thy wonderful works which thou hast done" (Psalm 40:5).